For those of us who want to hear *"...well done, good [...] joy of your Master" (Matthew 25:23)* this is a book for y[...] is a simple guide to help you navigate your part in [...] life to run the race with purpose and fulfillment. [...] [...] has written a guideline to help you recognize and implement the process of the key ingredients for the journey from revelation of your purpose and calling to reaching and fulfilling God's plan and destiny for you. It doesn't matter your age or position in life. It is never too late to align or realign to reach God's destiny for you!

*Jeremiah 29: 11 "For I know the thoughts and plans that I have for you, says the Lord, thoughts and plans for welfare and peace and not for evil, to give you hope in your final outcome." (AMPC)*

### Dr. John M. Benefiel
*Presiding Apostle, Heartland Apostolic Prayer Network*
*Founder and Senior Pastor, Church on the Rock, Oklahoma City*

Dr. Miller Bargeron's book entitled, *Journey of a Successful Dreamer*, is truly a breath of fresh air. He clearly and thoughtfully lays out some very real steps in pursuing one's God given dream. This is a time where so many people, even Christians, seem to be floundering around with no purpose and no direction. Dr. Bargeron provides a step by step blueprint in identifying and pursuing a life of purpose. As he states, *"Your gifts and talents are crying out to you. Use me! Use me! Please put me to work."* This is a sentiment that resonates in the hearts and minds of most people. The concepts are very well articulated, and there is a high level of scholarship within the book. Even so, I believe that it can be very easily understood by people at many levels. I can see this book as assisting many, both old and young, to not only identify but to be able to plan and to execute the fulfillment of their dream.

This book is a must read for anyone that desires to live a purpose driven life. Well Done!

### Joseph L Green Jr. M.A., PhD
*Commissioner, The 400-Year African American History Commission*
*Head Pastor, St. Paul Missionary Baptist Church*
*Founder, The 2019 Movement*

Dr. Miller Bargeron takes your hand...walking you, "Dreamer," with realistic practical steps through perhaps a "wilderness of delay"...into fulfillment of becoming a productive dreamer filled with "Wisdom" gained as you...Dream!

**Mama Bunny Warlan**
*HAPN, Global & 50 USA States Redemptive Gift Specialists*
*HAPN, Kentucky State Director*
*RPN, Kentucky State Director*

*Ecclesiastes 1:9 (ISV) "Whatever has happened will happen again."* Once again the Spirit of God has pierced the heart of a man and blessed us with a detailed guide for a successful life.

**Bishop Carl E. Grigsby**
*Christ Watch, The Ministry Corporation*

Miller Bargeron has invested his life creating intellectual properties. His expertise has once again proven itself. As a filmmaker, we often look for the finest writers to create films from their stories and writings. Miller combines an academic understanding and emotional balance to every story. It is my honor to highly recommend this amazing continuation in the works of this gifted writer into the industry.

**Dr. Kevin McAfee**
*Filmmaker, McAfee & Associates*

# JOURNEY OF A
# SUCCESSFUL DREAMER

## MILLER BARGERON, JR.

ISBN: 978-1-7350004-0-4

Printed in the United States of America


Cover Photo By: Tonya L. Moody and Shawn Bulloch

Graphic Design: Kennedy Talisa Bargeron

Cover Design By: Crystal Clear Creations

Formatted By: Crystal Clear Publishing

Edited By: Rebecca Bishopriggs, Jan Kelly, and Vikke Kearse Bargeron


For ordering information contact:

Scribe Tree Publishing

Scribe Tree Publishing, LLC

463 Pooler Parkway

Suite 207

Pooler, GA 31322


**www.millerbargeron.com**

# ABOUT THE AUTHOR

## Miller Bargeron, Jr., M.Th, D.CLM

In the essence of a renaissance man, Miller Bargeron, Jr. employs his abilities as a filmmaker, speaker, writer, and teacher to enlighten and empower individuals to achieve greater levels of understanding and success in their lives.

He is an award-winning film director and producer, having won an Africa Movie Academy Award (African Oscar) for the film "Stubborn as a Mule!" and several other national and international awards. Also, Miller is the managing partner of We Came to Conquer Entertainment, LLC, which he co-founded with his wife, Vikke Kearse Bargeron.

A dynamic speaker, Miller utilizes "Mindset Integration" as he engages in leadership and life navigation topics to help individuals make better choices leading to greater achievements in life. Miller is an award-winning screenplay writer having won an American Movie Award for the screenplay "Their Souls Cried Out." He has also co-authored two books: *To Redeem a Generation: African American Male Crisis* and *Keturah Revealed: Discovering Your Jewish Roots Workbook*.

Additionally, Miller is an ordained minister and commissioned Apostle. He and Vikke established Kingdom Bible Equipping and Training (KBET) and Youth Equipping and Training (YET). KBET and YET are ministries focused on teaching, training, and equipping adults, and youth, respectively, to live successful and spiritually grounded lives. Miller also serves as a member of the New Gate Apostolic Governing Board, and he is a board member of the 2019 Movement.

Miller has earned a Bachelor of Business Administration in Accounting, a Bachelor of Christian Leadership, a Master of Theology, and a Doctorate of

Christian Leadership and Management. In 2015, Miller was commissioned as an Ambassador of World Peace under the iChange Nations organization. Because of his humanitarian voice through film, Miller also received the Golden Rule International Award from iChange Nations in 2015 and a Global Leadership Award from iChange Nations in 2016. In addition, Miller has received an honorary Doctorate of Christian Arts and Entertainment and several other awards and honors.

In conjunction with all of his endeavors, Miller is also a very loving husband and dedicated father of three daughters, Kearsetyn, Kennedy, and Kerringtyn.

# DEDICATION

This book is dedicated to my loving, beautiful wife, Vikke, who has stood by me, supported me, encouraged me, interceded for me, and most of all loved me through my various journeys over our 23 plus years of marriage. Without you Bae, there would be no me. We are one in this journey of life. I love you so much.

# FOREWARD

This is a must read for individuals who are interested in fulfilling their destiny and purpose in life. Destiny is the necessary events that need to happen for a particular person or thing to perpetuate future advancement. Purpose is the reason for which something is created or exists. It seems that once a person positions himself to follow his destiny, and do the things necessary to get there, he can become successful. Whether it is through formal education, life skills education, career training, continuing education, or life experiences, we are all on some type of journey. It would be easier to discover our purpose if we follow the right steps of destiny to get us there. Purpose is why a person exists, it is why a person is alive, and it is what a person is created to do. We are in a time where purpose and destiny are kissing.

Dr. Bargeron is clearly calling all of us to consider a mindset change to help us become successful and fulfill our dreams. There are many great books about dreams, but Dr. Bargeron brings a greater insight with an understanding I haven't seen before. Most of us are not fulfilling our dreams because we have allowed fear to grip us. Dr. Bargeron's acronym C.H.A.N.G.E., Complete Happiness After Never Giving-up Expectations, is definitely a fresh formula for anyone to see their dream come to reality. *Journey of a Successful Dreamer* is a great book for people who have dreams, who want to dream, and those who have even been afraid to dream. This book will help us dream, and give us the necessary step by step tools to see our dreams fulfilled. You could be one step away from your dream being a reality. I encourage you to read, re-read, take notes, meditate, ponder, and review this book because it is a game changer for making all of your life's dreams a reality. Dare to dream!

**Dr. Venessa Battle**
US Chancellor, Kingdom Covenant Leadership Institute

# CONTENTS

# PREFACE

*Let me open my eyes so I can see,*

*The blessing that has been declared for me.*

*My journey has been set with lessons to learn,*

*Just open my eyes and fear not my earthly concerns.*

*Though the road may seem long and the path straight and narrow,*

*I will float through any valley of death like a targeted arrow.*

*With faith in my heart and destiny set as my course,*

*I will press toward my mark avoiding any future remorse.*

## OPEN YOUR EYES SO YOU CAN SEE YOUR DREAM

It is a dream that is full of **V.I.S.I.O.N.** (Victorious Insightful Strategies Illuminating Opportunities Nearby) waiting to unveil the success that only you can achieve. You have gifts and talents that are lying dormant within you. Their usefulness is drying up and withering away as they await your activation. Just like muscles that are unable to move after long periods of inactivity, your gifts and talents are experiencing atrophy.

These attributes are crying out to you. *"Use me! Use me! Please put me to work. Allow me to be a blessing to you and many others. Let me help you break the cycle of the redundant 9 to 5, the unfulfilled day to day, and the endless search for a better way of living. Let me help you rewire the reset button that you press every Sunday night before you go to bed. Let me cross up the polarities on your reset button and give you a jolt that will push you into a prosperous life."*

Years ago, my wife, Vikke, would drive our oldest daughter, Kearsetyn, to her piano lesson accompanied by our middle daughter, Kennedy. The ride to the lesson was normally 35 to 45 minutes, so the girls had an opportunity to take a nap on the way. One particular Wednesday afternoon, while on the ride to the piano lesson, Kennedy woke up frightened and screaming. Vikke quickly asked, "What is wrong Kennedy?" Kennedy's reply was, "Mommy, I was having a bad dream, and it scared me." Of course, Kennedy did not go back to sleep during that ride.

You may be thinking, *"What is unusual about a child waking up from a dream that turned into a nightmare?"* You are right; nothing is out of the ordinary. However, God gave me a revelation about my daughter's dream during a speech that I was giving to a group of college students. During the speech, I was talking about pursuing one's dream and oddly enough, I began telling the students about my daughter's nightmare. As I talked, the revelation started unfolding, so I said something along these lines:

*"While my child was sleeping, she started dreaming. Unfortunately, the dream took what she perceived to be a wrong turn, and it became a nightmare. Therefore, my daughter woke up feeling startled and afraid, and she never went back to sleep to finish dreaming.*

*Just like my daughter waking up from her dream, you may have awakened from yours, but not in the same sense. Many of you may have experienced this startled awakening. You started following your lifelong dream, but you ran into some unexpected situations and became afraid.*

*As your pursuit continued, those unexpected situations appeared to be looming nightmares that you did not want to face. So you stopped pursuing your dream because the fear of the unknown was greater than your desire to follow your dream through to completion."*

Unfortunately, this is not an unusual occurrence. Many people do not complete their lifelong dream. Better yet, most of them never attempt to pursue it. The interesting thing about dreaming is that you cannot control it. You can only follow it through to the end. However, the pursuit of a dream in life affords an individual more control via their choices. One of the biggest choices that can be made is choosing to move forward in spite of your fears. A wise person once said, *"I think I am going to run on to see what the end will be."* I am sorry to say that most people have never taken heed to that wisdom. Most people have stopped running or never even made it to the starting block all because of fear.

Unlike natural sleeping where you close your eyes to dream, you have to open your eyes to follow your life's quest. When you are afraid of something coming into your path, the natural reaction is to stop moving, close your eyes until the perceived danger has passed, or run away. This is the same reaction most people tend to have when they are pursuing their life's dream, and an unexpected situation appears in their path. They stop pursing the opportunity to obtain their dream, close their eyes (hesitate) and miss the opportunity, or they run away from.

So once again I say, OPEN YOUR EYES, SO YOU CAN SEE YOUR DREAM. In order to fulfill your dream, you must be able to see it unfold. While your eyes are closed, you miss many lessons that you must learn during the pursuit of your quest. When you stop moving in pursuit of it, you never see the blessings that are ahead of you. As you run away from unexpected situations, you never see the people and things that are already in the midst of the unexpected situation. These people and things are there to help you successfully navigate through the situation.

As you read this book, I will share with you the lessons that I have learned from studying the life of one of the greatest successful dreamers of all times; Joseph, the son of Jacob, the grandson of Isaac, and the great-grandson of Abraham. While studying Joseph's dramatic *Journey* to the fulfillment of his childhood dream, which ultimately led to him becoming second in charge in all the land of Egypt, a wonderful diagram for success was revealed to me. This diagram for success transcends its biblical boundaries of Old Testament splendor and stands strong as present-day principles that will guide you on your *Journey of a Successful Dreamer.*

3

# JOSEPH

## A SYNOPSIS OF A SUCCESSFUL DREAMER

(Genesis 37-47)

The biblical story of Joseph opens with Joseph as a seventeen year old lad working faithfully in his father's business. Joseph's father was Jacob, who was the son of Isaac and the grandson of Abraham, the patriarch of the Hebrews. Joseph was his father's favorite son because he was born in Jacob's elder years. However, Jacob's favoritism brought about the hatred of his other sons toward Joseph. Jacob made it worse by displaying his love of Joseph by giving him a beautiful coat of many colors. In addition to the hatred of Joseph's brothers toward him, Joseph had two dreams that showed him the vision for his life. This was his *Dream Presentation.* However, his family members did not embrace or receive his dreams. As a matter of fact, his brothers hated him more because of his dreams.

In great excitement, Joseph told his brothers his first dream. He said, *"There we were, binding sheaves in the field. Then behold, my sheaf arose and also stood upright; and indeed your sheaves stood all around and bowed down to my sheaf." (Genesis 37:7 – NKJV)* Of course, Joseph's brothers did not like what they heard. Nevertheless, Joseph anxiously told his brothers the second dream when it occurred. He told them, *"...Look, I have dreamed another dream. And this time, the sun, the moon, and the eleven stars bowed down to me." (Genesis 37:9 – NKJV)* Essentially, the dreams were indicating that Joseph would one day be in authority over his family, and they would have to bow down to him.

After telling his brothers the second dream, Joseph told his father about his dreams. Jacob immediately reprimanded him for the dreams and said,

5

*"...What is this dream that you have dreamed? Shall your mother and I and your brothers indeed come to bow down to the earth before you?" (Genesis 37:10 – NKJV)* Although Jacob rebuked Joseph, he did not dismiss the vision in Joseph's dreams. However, Joseph's brothers envied him even more.

A short time after Joseph's *Dream Presentation*, his brothers came together and plotted to kill him in order to stop his *Dream Fulfillment*. His brothers had a meeting and said, *"Come now, let's kill him and throw him into one of these cisterns and say that a ferocious animal devoured him. Then we'll see what comes of his dreams." (Genesis 37:20 – NIV)* However, one of his brothers, Reuben, called for mercy on Joseph's life and said, *"...Shed no blood, but cast him into this pit which is in the wilderness, and do not lay a hand on him..." (Genesis 37:22 – NKJV)* As a result, Joseph's *Wilderness March* began. This is the part of his *Journey* that would prepare him for his *Dream Fulfillment.*

Joseph's brothers proceeded with their plan and threw him into an empty pit with no food or water. Before they cast him into the pit, they removed his coat of many colors. Meanwhile, a group of Ishmealites was traveling towards them. Judah, one of the brothers, had a bright idea. He thought that it would profit them more to sell Joseph to the Ishmaelites as a slave. In doing this, their brother's blood would not be on their hands. So they sold Joseph to the Ishmaelites for twenty pieces of silver, and the Ishmaelites took Joseph into Egypt with them.

After Joseph was carried off into bondage, his brothers returned home to their father. They presented Jacob with Joseph's coat, which they had ripped into pieces and covered with animal blood. They told their father that Joseph had been devoured by an evil beast. Jacob was greatly grieved by the loss of his son. Meanwhile, the Ishmaelites completed their trip to Egypt. When they arrived, they sold Joseph to Potiphar, who was one of Pharaoh's officers and the captain of the guard.

Even though it appeared that Joseph was dealt a bad hand to play in life, he accepted his hand and worked as a faithful servant unto Potiphar. As Joseph served Potiphar, God honored his faithfulness by making all of his endeavors successful. Because of the favor of God, Potiphar took notice of Joseph and promoted him to manager over all he had. As a result, Potiphar's household and business affairs were blessed.

After some time had passed, Potiphar's wife also took notice of Joseph. However, she was not drawn to Joseph because of his faithfulness. Her attraction was lust. On many occasions, she asked Joseph to be intimate with her. In every instance, Joseph resisted her seduction and maintained his integrity by refusing her advances. In the course of time, Joseph told Potiphar's wife, "…*Look, my master does not know what is with me in the house, and he has committed all that he has to my hand. There is no one greater in this house than I, nor has he kept back anything from me but you, because you are his wife. How then can I do this great wickedness, and sin against God?" (Genesis 39:8-9– NKJV)*

Potiphar's wife could not bear the rejection, so one day she decided to be vindictive. She made one of her normal seductive advances, but this time she grabbed Joseph by his outer garment. Being the man that he was, Joseph refused her once again and pulled away from her by taking off his garment. Subsequently, Potiphar's wife called some of the other men that worked in the house and accused Joseph of trying to seduce her. She showed the men Joseph's garment as proof of her accusation.

When Potiphar returned home, his wife told him the lie and showed him the garment. Potiphar became enraged, immediately throwing Joseph into the prison where Pharaoh kept his prisoners. However, the favor of God shined on Joseph even in prison. After being incarcerated for a short while, the Head Jailer grew to like Joseph, so he placed him in charge of all the inmates.

After time had passed, Pharaoh had his personal baker and butler imprisoned for offending him. Coincidently, they were placed in the section of the prison where Joseph was located. One night, the butler and the baker had perplexing dreams they could not understand. The next morning, Joseph found the two men in a state of confusion, and he prayed to God on their behalf for an interpretation.

The interpretation of the butler's dream was that in three days he would be restored back to his former position as Pharaoh's butler. Perceiving a possible "get out of jail" card, Joseph asked the butler not to forget about him when he saw Pharaoh again. The baker's dream was not so pleasant because it indicated that in three days Pharaoh was going to hang him. Within three days, both of Joseph's interpretations proved to be accurate, but the butler forgot to mention Joseph to Pharaoh upon his return to the palace.

After about two years of faithfully enduring his false imprisonment, Joseph was finally going to be rewarded for his steadfastness. As it would happen, Pharaoh had two disturbing dreams that were so perplexing that not even his wise men or magicians could explain. This was truly a moment when God was going to take a bad incident and turn it into something great. When the butler heard about Pharaoh's situation, he remembered Joseph's gift of interpretation and immediately told Pharaoh.

In order to ease Pharaoh's mind, Joseph was released from prison so he could interpret the dreams. Before entering the palace, he had to be made presentable by being shaved, bathed, and dressed in clean clothes. When Joseph entered Pharaoh's presence, Pharaoh told him about his dreams and asked if he understood them. Joseph humbly answered him by saying, "...*It is not in me; God will give Pharaoh an answer of peace.*" *(Genesis 41:16– NKJV)*

Once Joseph heard the entire dream, he told Pharaoh that God was showing him that the land of Egypt was going to experience seven years of plentiful crops and seven years of subsequent famine. Not only did God allow Joseph to interpret the dreams, He also gave Joseph instructions on how Pharaoh needed to manage the seven years of plenty in order to survive the seven years of famine.

Upon hearing the interpretation of the dreams and the ensuing instructions, Pharaoh accepted what Joseph told him. He immediately made a decision that he needed to put a man in position to carry out what God had instructed. As a result, Pharaoh appointed Joseph to fulfill this position which made him ruler over the land of Egypt. Who else could better fill such a role? The only person that would be higher than Joseph would be Pharaoh himself. Seven years of plenty came and passed, and Joseph did as God instructed. As a result, the land of Egypt had an abundance of corn to last for more than the seven years of famine. However, the other nations around Egypt did not fare so well with their crops before the famine. All of the other nations had to go to Egypt to buy corn, even the land of Canaan where Joseph's family lived. At the time of Joseph's promotion, he was 30 years old.

As the seven years of famine began, Jacob, Joseph's father, sent his sons to Egypt to buy corn. Because Joseph was the ruler of all the land of Egypt, his brothers had to go before him to ask to purchase corn. When the brothers came before him, they had to bow down and ask for corn. Joseph immediately knew who they were, but they did not recognize him. Knowing as such, he did not tell them who he was as he began treating them harshly. He even accused them of being spies for Canaan. Nevertheless, Joseph eventually blessed them by filling their sacks with corn for free, and he gave them provisions to make their trip back to Canaan. At that time, the brothers were not aware of his kindness unto them. Although he never revealed himself to his brothers, he did remember his dreams. Joseph had just experienced his *Dream Fulfillment*.

Upon returning to Canaan, the brothers opened their sacks and found all of their money there, along with the corn. They did not know what to think, so they immediately went to Jacob and told him what had happened.

As time passed, the famine continued. So Jacob told his sons to return to Egypt and purchase more corn. When they arrived in Egypt, Joseph had them brought to his house for dinner. While they were in the house, Joseph set them up to be accused of stealing which made them afraid for their lives. In a state of fear, they pleaded their innocence. The brothers talked about how their father's heart was broken after they lied to him about Joseph being killed by an evil beast. They stated how Jacob would not be able to withstand losing any more sons. They also exclaimed their sorrow and remorse for selling Joseph into slavery.

After taking his brothers through a lot of grief, Joseph started feeling guilty and overwhelmed with emotions. Suddenly, he broke down and told his brothers that he was Joseph, their brother whom they sold into slavery. The brothers were greatly troubled, and they felt even more remorseful. Joseph immediately forgave them and told them not to be grieved nor angry with themselves. He further said that God had sent him to Egypt in order to save lives. At that point, the purpose for all of Joseph's trials was revealed. If Joseph had not gone on his *Journey*, many people in many nations would have died because of the famine.

After an emotional reunion, Joseph told his brothers to return home and tell their father that he was alive and that God had made him lord of all Egypt. Joseph also told them to pack up the family, and move them all to Egypt to live out the famine. As a show of support, Pharaoh sent chariots back with the brothers to move Jacob and the family to Egypt. Joseph was finally reunited with his family, and they lived in Egypt under Joseph's prosperity.

In the pursuit of your dream, life can come at you fast and furiously. One moment, everything appears to be functioning fine and conveniently structured. The next moment, your life may seem to have quickly turned upside down and chaotic. It is as though someone looked into the pretty glass globe that is your life and decided to pick it up, turn it over, and shake it up. Now all you can see are big white balls of snow furiously rushing at you. In the midst of the shaking, you may not be able to see the purpose for the disruption. Nevertheless, you have to faithfully stay on your path, knowing that the snow will settle, and your world will once again be a pretty picture to behold.

As you begin your *Journey* toward your *Dream Fulfillment*, the snow will fall and cover your path. It will freeze and kill those things in your life that are hindering your growth, and it will preserve you as you grow and mature into who God has called you to be. Once the snow melts away, a new person will emerge; a person who is walking in their fulfilled dream. This is what Joseph experienced on his *Journey* to becoming ruler of Egypt, and this is what you will experience on your *Journey of a Successful Dreamer.*

# INTRODUCTION

*I have a vision of what my life can be,*

*Even though making it a reality has been really hard for me.*

*Today I stand in great disarray,*

*I cannot help but feel my dreams are fading away.*

*For some strange reason,*

*I seem to be stuck in a dry season.*

*Can someone help me find my way?*

I t is wonderful how the lives of successful individuals are displayed via the many media outlets such as radio, print, internet, and television. These mediums allow us to see their successes, one after another. However, the prevailing question is always, "How did they become successful?" Even though documentaries have been produced, and books have been written on many successful individuals, none of these discourses tend to tell the full *Journey* of the individual's success. You might hear a story or two about how they grew up, and the opportunities that catapulted them into success, but the stories never give enough details to lead you down your path to success.

Unfortunately, this display of success can have an adverse effect on most individuals. You can become so intrigued with other people's success that you continually watch their successes and forget about creating your own successful life. I will not lie. I was guilty of this at one time. I found myself always watching television shows like "E! True Hollywood Stories" or "Biography." I was subliminally trying to live vicariously through other successful people. However, I quickly realized that a surrogate life through someone else would never give me the true happiness and gratification that I desired. I began telling myself, *"You will never see your life story on television; nor will you find success if you continually watch everyone else's life story."*

My vision was not about being on television. It was about having such an empowering effect on the lives of others that the various media sources deemed my story worth sharing. That is the main reason why the lives of successful people are displayed. Their life, whether it made someone smile, laugh, or make a change for the better, made a difference in the lives of other people. An individual's success is not for themselves only, but their success should be about how their life empowers other people. That cannot be accomplished by sitting around and watching another person's success. Therefore, my mindset and my actions had to change. I had to begin my *Journey* toward fulfilling my dream.

One day, I was walking around the office looking for my manager. However she was squatting by an employee's cubical having a conversation. Keep in mind, she is about 5' 2" tall. It actually did not matter if she were standing, sitting, or squatting, I would not have been able to see her over the 5' 6" cubicle walls. So I had to go aisle by aisle looking for her.

When I found her, I said in a joking manner, *"Oh, there you are, I could not see you over the cubicle walls."* She laughed and said, *"Very funny."* She knew I was referring to her height more so than the fact that she was squatting. Being the high-energy person she is, she proceeded to kneel on a file cabinet. The height of the file cabinet allowed her to see eye to eye with me as well as look around the office the way I do, standing 6' 2" tall. She immediately said, *"Wow, you can see everything from up here.*

All of a sudden, the file cabinet became unstable. After looking over the cubical, she grabbed hold of the adjacent cubical wall. She said, *"Whoa! How do you do this?"* She was actually joking about me being tall enough to look over the cubicle. I told her, *"When I look over the cubical walls, I am standing on my own two feet, but you are kneeling on a cabinet."* At that time, my statement really did not prompt any thought. However, God brought it back to my remembrance, and I saw the symbolic meaning behind it.

When you are able to look at life the way someone else sees it, his or her vantage point initially appears to be exciting and manageable. At first glance, you may think that you are able to handle their altitude of sight. However, you quickly realize that another person's vantage point is not exactly what you think it is. What you see from their vantage point is not your reality. Furthermore, another person's reality is never a stable environment for you. The only stable environment is one that you build while standing on your own two feet, not riding the back of another person's vision. Looking at another person's success, or even partaking in another person's accomplishment is not the same as walking in your own successful life.

# C.H.A.N.G.E.

In the early 1990's, a famous hip hop and R&B music producer co-wrote and produced a hit song for the famous gospel group, The Winans. The name of the song was simply titled, "It's Time." The part of the song that resonates in my mind the most is the chorus:

> *"It's time, time to make a change,*
>
> *We are His people; we can do it."*

Not only were the lyrics powerful, but the combination of a hip hop/R&B producer collaborating with a gospel group was a big change that led to a current day trend. These profound lyrics still hold resounding power today. It is time for you to make a change in your life, and I know you can do it.

You must first transform your mindset to change your life. Such a move will not only mark a turning point in your life, but *C.H.A.N.G.E.* is what will fuel your *Journey* to fulfilling your dream. *C.H.A.N.G.E.* is an acronym for Complete Happiness After Never Giving-up Expectations. An individual is only completely happy when they receive everything they expect. Anything short of those expectations will be settling for less, and if you settle for less, you will likely have a "what if complex" the rest of your life. What if I had done this? What if I had done that?

As you begin the *Journey* toward fulfilling your dream, you must believe it will come true. You have to expect that it will one day be a reality no matter what it may be. However, your *Journey* must be filled with reasonable and obtainable expectations. I am not saying do not shoot for the moon. I am simply saying set up your expectations in obtainable stages. Before you shoot for the moon, you should do the following: 1) learn how to fly, 2) purchase a space shuttle, and 3) plan your trip. As you accomplish each stage, you draw closer to complete happiness. The key is never giving up on your expectations.

As you journey toward the fulfillment of your dream, you will find that change is inevitable in your quest. The modifications that are required will be necessary for you to operate in and sustain your dream.

## WHAT IS YOUR DREAM?

A *dream* is defined as a fond hope, aspiration, or vision. I specifically like the term *vision* which is defined as something seen by other than normal sight. The word vision is truly indicative of our life's dream. In its simplest form, your dream can be revealed in a quiet night's sleep. In a more complex manner, it can be revealed through a series of good or bad events that conclude with your desire to fulfill a need. As a result, for unidentifiable reasons, you are continually drawn to fulfilling that need. That pulling you feel is like a homing beacon that draws you to your life's dream.

My question to you is what is your dream? What is it that you want to do in life? What is that one thing that keeps calling your name? What is that one thing that you cannot get out of your mind? What is that one thing that has left an indelible impression on you? Chances are that "thing" is your dream, or it is closely connected to your dream. If none of these questions apply to you at this time, do not worry, they will at some point because your prosperous life is connected to your dream. You just have to follow the homing beacon when you feel it drawing you.

Believe it or not, we all have a dream living inside of us. Our dream ultimately contains the secrets of living a successful life. However, most people never recognize it, or they allow it to lay dormant inside of them and never live life to their fullest potential. People do not follow their dreams for many reasons, but most of them can be associated with some type of fear. However, you must conquer your fears and give your dream a chance at becoming your reality.

Picture in your mind a long, narrow, red ladder that touches the ground ten feet in front of you. As you stare up the ladder, it appears to reach up to heaven. At the same time, the steps of the ladder seem to disappear as you look up toward the top of it. The disappearing steps seem to make it impossible to reach the top. However, approaching the ladder and taking one step up at a time will eventually get you there. As you take each step, your ascent becomes clearer and easier. Eventually, you find yourself at the top of the ladder.

Think about it for a moment. The red ladder represents the *Journey* to your dream, and the beginning of it has been right in front of your face. Unfortunately, you have been afraid to move toward it, even though your dream at the end of the *Journey* looks like heaven. Nevertheless, you could not clearly see each step of the journey, which preempted your attempt to go after your dream. So you gave up the pursuit of your dream.

Today, I want to encourage you to take that first step toward your dream. Every step you take will clarify your vision and make your *Journey* a little easier. I will admit, the course of getting to your dream at the top of the ladder may be hard. However, I want to share with you a process for manifesting your dream. I call this process the *Journey of a Successful Dreamer.*

# LET YOUR JOURNEY BEGIN

Whenever you embark on any journey, you must complete three different stages to be successful. The three stages are: 1) determining a destination, 2) mapping and traveling the path to your destination, and 3) reaching the destination. The *Journey of a Successful Dreamer* follows that same process.

First, the destination or the dream has to be defined. This stage is called the *Dream Presentation*. The second stage is called the *Wilderness March;* it is the most important part of the *Journey*. The *Wilderness March* prepares and/or matures you for the manifestation of your dream. The last stage is the *Dream Fulfillment* which is where you start operating within the full scope of your dream.

Now that you know the process to achieving your dream, it is time to begin your *Journey* to becoming a *Successful Dreamer.*

# STAGE I

# DREAM PRESENTATION

Where does it all begin? When will I receive my dream? When will my big revelation occur? Chances are you have probably seen at least a glimpse of it. You may have noticed that you have certain affinities to activities or ideas you have never been exposed to. You may be wondering why you are drawn to ventures that are not a part of your normal routine, but for some reason you feel good whenever you think about them.

What you are experiencing is a partial reception from the signal emanating from your dream's homing beacon. However, the signal has been faint and intermittent because you have not been in the right position, or you will not stay in the right position long enough to receive a clear signal. I will explain more about the right position in a moment.

Believe it or not, we all have a dream homing beacon that is or will be drawing, pulling, coercing, and begging us to follow it. That signal will ultimately lead us to fulfilling our dreams in life. For some people, their signal started calling them at an early age, while others do not receive a signal until later in life. In either case, your dreams are for a specific time of your life. Therefore, your *Dream Presentation* will begin at a point in your life where you will have ample time to complete the necessary *Journey* to mature, or become prepared to fulfill your dream.

The signal that is being transmitted is from God. It is calling out to a receiver that He placed in you when you were born into the earth realm. In Jeremiah 1:5 (NKJV), God told Jeremiah the following:

*"Before I formed you in the womb I knew you;*

*before you were born I sanctified you;*

*I ordained you a prophet to the nations."*

*God further stated in Jeremiah 29:11 (NIV):*

*"For I know the plans I have for you," declares the Lord,*

*"plans to prosper you and not to harm you,*

*plans to give you hope and a future."*

From the beginning of your existence, God placed a dream inside of you. One of the definitions of the word dream is a fond hope. God told Jeremiah that he was birthed with plans that would give him a hope and a future. You are no different from Jeremiah. God has placed a dream inside of you that will give you a future worth hoping for and a future full of prosperity. Unfortunately, many individuals continually ignore or overlook the signal from their homing beacon. Consequently, they never obtain the prosperity that is declared theirs at birth.

It is time to tune into your dream's signal!

## STOP AND BE STILL

Have you ever taken a trip by car, and began listening to your favorite radio station? As you continue driving, you get to that point where the strength of the radio station's transmitter begins to fade. Eventually, you travel far enough away from the radio station that your car radio, which is a receiver, loses the signal. When this occurs, the only way to begin receiving the signal again is to travel back toward the radio station.

Just like the car radio, you may be losing your dream's signal, or you may have already lost it. In order to regain the signal, you must turn around and go back toward your dream's homing beacon. Even though it may seem difficult to hone in on it at first, as you get closer, it will become easier to follow the direction of the signal. But how far have you ventured away from your signal?

Where were you when you were last able to receive your dream's signal? What were you doing when you last received it and whose leadership were you under? Was it strong or weak? These are important questions to ask yourself because returning to the signal from your dream is not as easy as tuning into the signal from your favorite radio station. When it comes to a radio signal, you know the location of the transmission. On the other hand, you have yet to find or fulfill your dream, so you do not know the location of your dream's homing beacon. Therefore, you must stop moving and be still. The further you travel away from your dream's signal, the harder it is to find it because the reception has been lost.

The correlation between a radio station's signal and your dream's homing beacon actually gets more interesting. Have you ever noticed that in the still of the night, you can sometimes pick up radio stations that you cannot receive during the busyness of the day? When that occurs, and you like what you hear, you tend to lock into that radio station and listen to it. The signal from your dream is similar. In the still of the night, while you are thinking or sleeping, sometimes you start receiving the signal from your dream. When that occurs, you need to lock in and follow it.

## BE FAITHFUL

Listen closely. The next few sentences are paramount. I do not want you to miss a key ingredient to becoming a *Successful Dreamer*. Earlier, when I said be still, I did not mean to stand still and do nothing. On the contrary, I mean for you to be patient and faithful in whatever your current assignment happens to be. Your current assignment could be your existing place of employment, the school where you are presently enrolled, or your current position in ministry, just to name a few.

In whatever assignment God has placed you, be faithful. If you hate your job, and you cannot wait to work at your dream career or in your own business, be faithful where you are. Be the best at your current position. If you are enrolled in a school where you feel you are not being challenged or trained properly, be faithful where you are, and make the best grades until you are accepted at the school of your choice. If you are the CD duplicator in your church ministry, and you know God has called you to preach, be faithful where you are until your time of elevation comes.

Simply stated, your faithfulness in your current assignment is the key that will unlock your *Dream Presentation* when that time comes. In Matthew 25, Jesus gives a prolific message about being faithful in your current assignment in His teaching on the "Parable of the Talents." The 21ˢᵗ verse of Matthew 25 (NKJV) states:

> *"…Well done, good and faithful servant;*
>
> *you were faithful over a few things,*
>
> *I will make you ruler over many things.*
>
> *Enter into the joy of your lord."*

In order for your dream to be revealed, you have to prove that you can be faithful over your current assignment.

As you operate faithfully in your existing assignment, you become more receptive to your dream's signal. Eventually, it becomes so strong that it manifests in a vision. In your vision, you will see the fulfillment of your dream. Your vision may be revealed during the quiet of a night's sleep, or it could be revealed in a midday's moment that you have stolen from the hustle

21

of a busy work schedule. In either case, it marks the *Dream Presentation* stage of your *Journey of a Successful Dreamer.*

In order to start any journey, you must have a destination in mind. Through your *Dream Presentation,* you now have a destination set. However, your *Dream Presentation* never shows you the path you will have to travel to fulfill your dream. Your path will be established by the amount and type of preparation you will need to operate in the full scope of your dream. This is a part of destination mapping, which I will talk about that in Stage II of the *Journey.*

## THE RIGHT POSITION

Believe it or not, your faithful execution of your current assignment is setting you up to fulfill your dream. Remember, it is about being in the right position to receive your signal. Just as you must be in the right position to receive your dream's signal, you also must be in the right position to efficiently begin your *Journey of a Successful Dreamer.*

As an illustration, imagine that you have planned a driving trip to New York (NY) to pick up your grandmother-in-law. She wants to spend the summer with your family in Georgia (GA). About a week before you plan to leave for NY, some unexpected developments occur, and you have to make a trip to Mississippi (MS) to wrap up some business. Due to time restraints, you now have to drive to NY from MS instead of driving from GA. As a result of being away from home, your jaunt to NY is going to cost you more time and more money.

In the same sense, being out of the right position during your *Dream Presentation* causes your *Journey* to fulfilling your dream to take longer and may cost you more. In other words, your position at the time you begin your *Journey* has a big effect on your path to fulfilling your dream. God is going to reveal your dream in His appointed time so that you will be prepared to walk in the fullness of it. Meanwhile, He will do whatever is necessary to keep you on His schedule. When you are not in the right position during your *Dream Presentation*, God will orchestrate your life to get you back in the proper place--that is, if you trust Him.

You are probably thinking more about your right position because it has such a great bearing on your life. Believe it or not, the right position is a lot more than being in a specific place. It is a coordinating voyage that is woven into the architecture of your *Journey of a Successful Dreamer*. It is like a sub-plot in your dream. The right position consists of a series of three chain Reactive Actions that will propel you through your *Journey of a Successful Dreamer*. The three Reactive Actions coincide with the three stages of your *Journey*. The actions are reactive because they are predicated on prior events.

Your series of Reactive Actions will begin as soon as you receive your *Dream Presentation*. If you are in the right position, your movement through your *Journey* can be a lot less turbulent. If you are out of sync, your movement through your *Journey* will be a lot more turbulent than it has to be.

Being in the right position consists of three chain Reactive Action steps: Right Mindset, Right Place, and Right Time. All three of these steps build upon each other, creating a final reaction that thrusts you into your *Dream Fulfillment*. Your propulsion can be directional, or it can be widespread. A directional thrust will accomplish its goal with minimal loss to you because it follows one path. However, a widespread thrust may cause you massive losses because it has to cover a broader scope of positions. Such is the result of not staying in the right position.

## *Reactive Action #1 – The Right Mindset*

The first action, the right mindset, is pivotal. What is your mindset when you receive your *Dream Presentation*? Are you mentally mature enough to receive your life's destination? Does your mentality send you into deep thought about all of your assumed inadequacies? Does your mindset tell you that you cannot accomplish your dream because no one in your family has ever accomplished anything like your vision? Does your frame of mind send you into a deep state of fear? Or does your mindset prompt you to stand, and go get what was predestined to be yours at your birth?

The answers to the above questions are ultimately what will create the first reaction in your chain. If your reaction or mindset is negative, your *Journey* will take some unnecessary detours. However, if your mindset is positive, then your *Journey* will take a more direct path. Take note that I did not say a straight path. Many ups and downs are bound to occur on your *Journey*, because obtaining your dream will require some hard work on your part. However, a negative mindset will cause you to go back and forth over the same issues on your *Journey*, which only makes it harder.

As I was writing this section about mindsets, I thought about my daughter, Kennedy, and an experience she had during a doctor's visit. It was an annual well-child visit when she was about three years old. Unfortunately for my daughter, it was time for her to receive an immunization shot. Everything was going fine at first because she really loves her doctor. But when the nurse entered the room with the needle, all "you know what" broke loose!

My daughter started screaming like most children in that situation, and as usual, daddy had to be one of the bad guys, and hold his daughter in position to receive the shot. My daughter's mindset was obviously negative. She did not want any part of that shot and was determined to fight against receiving it with all her might, literally. Nevertheless, I held her in position for her to receive the shot. I, having the better understanding of the situation, had to make sure my daughter received the vaccination in order to prevent future illness. Although it was hard for her to endure, and even harder for me to see her endure, her future health was at stake.

As I held my daughter, the nurse proceeded to inject the medicine in her thigh. As soon as she felt the pain from the needle penetrating her skin, she immediately summoned some supernatural strength and speed, and snatched her arm away from me. Raking her hand toward her thigh, she knocked the needle out of the nurse's hand. Just that quickly she had jumped out of position. In the process, she created a one-inch scar from the needle dragging along her skin. Of course I consoled her and calmed her nerves, but I still had to get her back in position for the shot. She had to get her vaccination.

Fortunately, the second attempt went a lot smoother even though it was still painful. If she had the mindset to endure the vaccination the first time, (I know; big wish for a three-year-old), she could have experienced less turmoil and pain. Not only did she have to endure being stuck with a needle twice, she also had to deal with the pain of the one-inch scar as it healed. Now she has a constant reminder of her negative mindset on her thigh.

Getting the shot was inevitable, but how painful the shot would be was up to my daughter. The right mindset would have made the shot less painful, just like you having the right mindset will make your *Journey* less tumultuous.

## *Reactive Action #2 – The Right Place*

The second Reactive Action is being in the right place. Because this action has a direct tie to your current assignment, its success is totally dependent on your first Reactive Action. In most cases, your current assignment will be one of the least likely stops that you envisioned enroute to your *Dream Fulfillment*. However, your mindset, while you are in your current assignment, will determine how quickly you are promoted from that assignment to the next one. Whenever you are assigned to a place, certain tasks have to be accomplished before you can move on. Your mindset, while in that place, will either speed up the process or impede it.

When you are in the right place with the right mindset, the environmental variables that are needed for you to become a *Successful Dreamer* are attracted to you. These variables consist of people, money, knowledge, and any other resources that are needed to help you fulfill your *dream*. If you are diligent in working in your current assignment, the people that are assigned to help you fulfill your dream take notice of your work ethic, and consequently become interested in helping you accomplish bigger and better things.

Take for example Joseph, the poster child for the *Journey of a Successful Dreamer*. Joseph probably would have never guessed that in order for him to reach his *Dream Fulfillment*, he would have to spend years in prison because of a false accusation. Nevertheless, he maintained the proper mindset while in prison, and peacefully endured his sentence.

Moreover, Joseph's positive mindset transcended into the second reactive action, the right place. Because he was in the right place (which was prison), with the right mindset, he was able to be a blessing to Pharaoh's butler and baker when they were thrown into prison. As a result, Joseph made a lasting impression on the butler, which ultimately led to him becoming second in charge in Egypt.

Although you may not be in the most ideal place, endure it, and do your best to fulfill your assignment. You will be surprised to know who is taking notice of you and what type of resources they can provide for you.

## *Reactive Action #3 – The Right Time*

The final Reactive Action is the right time. Although you may have met the people you need to align with and have access to needed resources, the last part of the reactions in the series has to come to pass before you are catapulted into the right position. If you think of this action as a chemical reaction, a greater understanding can be grasped. When you combine various elements together to create a new chemical bond, a process has to occur. Although all of the elements are present in the mixture, a certain amount of time has to pass before the chemical bond can be completed. The amount of time needed depends on the complexity of the chemical bond.

When I was in high school, I took a required chemistry class. However, that class became more than just another class needed for graduation. I distinctly remember having to do an experiment with the element bromine. At that time, my lab partner was Allen, a good friend of mine. The lab assignment was to mix the elements bromine and iodine. Being the studious individuals that Allen and I were, we totally embraced our assignment.

As we mixed the bromine and the iodine together and added a catalytic agent, a chemical reaction started. Keep in mind, the catalytic agent ignited the reaction. Yet, the interesting thing about bromine and iodine is that they are halogens, which make them unique elements. Both of these elements stand out by themselves because they are brightly colored. Another characteristic of the elements is that bromine is a liquid while iodine is a chunky solid.

Once the catalyst ignited the reaction, the bromine and the iodine synthesized into a new compound, which was a type of bromide. Because this was not a complex chemical bond, it did not take much time to form. Nevertheless, two totally different elements came together and created a dynamic bond. Even though their characteristics were different, a synergistic reaction between the two elements created something new and good.

At the end of the experiment, Allen and I adopted a name for our friendship. We called ourselves the "Bromide Brothers" because that reaction described our relationship. We were two unique individuals that came together and created a dynamic bond that seemed inseparable.

In essence, this is what happens at the end of the three reactive actions that make up the right position. In order to create something new and good, which is ultimately your *Dream Fulfillment*, a synergy between the first two Reactive Actions, the right mindset and the right place, has to occur. Your outlook must be positive and embrace the place in which you are currently situated. In turn, this synergy allows the right time to be added to the equation, thus serving as a catalyst that will ignite your mindset and your resources. As a result, a reaction will occur that will create a new and good bond. This new bond will result in you walking in maturity and being prepared for your *Dream Fulfillment*.

# REVELATION VS. REALITY

Now that you have a clearer understanding of the *Dream Presentation*, I am going to give you some more knowledge about this initial stage of your *Journey*. As you have learned, you can make certain decisions after receiving your *Dream Presentation* that will make your *Journey* easier. In addition to what was previously mentioned, like having the right mindset and being faithful at your current assignment, two other areas must be incorporated: Revelation and Reality. When you receive your *Dream Presentation*, you must always embrace the revelatory aspects of your dream, as well as facing the reality of your dream.

## *Revelation*

Webster's Dictionary gives a basic definition of the word *revelation* as a revealing or disclosing of something. It also gives a reference to the word revelation in the context of Christian theology. It states that revelation is "God's disclosure or manifestation of Himself and His will." Under that correlation, your *Dream Presentation* is God showing you His will for your life. Just in case you do not remember, you have probably asked God for His will to be manifested in your life many times. So why is it that you ignore Him when He answers your petition? Let me help you. In Matthew 6:9-10 *(NKJV)*, Jesus stated the beginning of what is known as the "Our Father's Prayer":

> "...*Our Father in heaven, hallowed be your name,*
>
> *your Kingdom come; your will be done on earth as it is in heaven...*"

You have asked for God's will, i.e., your *Dream Presentation* to be manifested every time you prayed the "Our Father's Prayer." When the *Dream Presentation* is given, you have to properly handle the revelation that God has given for your life. There are actually three steps to managing a revelation from God. I call these three steps the Three R's of Revelation: Recognize, Receive, and Record.

When your dream is presented, you must recognize it for what it is. Your *Dream Presentation* reveals your destiny in life. Many people have stopped at this step because they did not recognize that the vision they saw was actually the fulfillment of their purpose in life. Therefore, they never attempt to embrace their vision as their life's dream. Recognition is a key component. If the key to your success is dangling in front of your face, yet you do not recognize it as such, that key is useless. Open your mind's eye, so you can see your dream.

The second step in managing your revelation is receiving the dream. Although some people recognize their vision as their purpose in life, they do not receive it as such for various reasons. When I say receive the dream, I mean embrace it. The various reasons people do not receive their dream are usually connected to some type of fear. For instance, they tend to have a fear of leaving their comfort zone, a fear of going against the opinions and ideas of family and friends, a fear of failing, or even a fear of succeeding. If you never embrace your dream, you will never realize that you are actually well suited and capable of fulfilling it.

How do you embrace your dream? You embrace it by following the path that you will encounter on your *Journey of a Successful Dreamer*. Whether your path seems doable or impossible, follow it faithfully. Then watch how everything comes together with the needed resources and how they work in harmony to accomplish your *Dream Fulfillment*.

In order to recognize and receive your dream, your mindset has to be in a positive state. When you get your vision, your psyche will have to connect with it and say, *"I can see myself fulfilling this dream."* Once you get past the recognition step, your mentality has to be strong enough to encourage you to not only begin your *Journey*, but to also complete your *Journey*. Without the right mindset, the steps to recognition and receive will never be taken.

The third step to managing your revelation is recording your *dream*, which has been an underrated step by many people. Thousands of years ago, Habakkuk, a minor prophet, and God had an interesting dialogue that drew emphasis on this step. This dialogue, found in the Old Testament, presents a lesson that is important for us to glean from.

In the book of Habakkuk, God gave him a revelation, but he became impatient while waiting on the manifestation of the revelation. However, Habakkuk eventually came to the realization that he had to wait and endure the process of manifesting the vision. Therefore, Habakkuk told God the following in chapter 2:1 (NKJV):

*"I will stand my watch*

*and set myself on the rampart,*

*and watch to see what He will say to me,*

*and what I will answer when I am corrected."*

When you look up the Hebrew meaning of the word *watch* in this verse, it is defined as a duty or an office. In other words, Habakkuk was telling God that he was going to stay at his current assignment until he heard from Him. As stated earlier, your current assignment is a key part of fulfilling your dream. Once Habakkuk decided to be faithful where he was stationed, God gave him more knowledge to continue on his *Journey.* In Habakkuk 2:2-3 (NIV), God told him the following:

*"Write down the revelation and make it plain on tablets*

*so that a herald may run with it. For the revelation awaits*

*an appointed time; it speaks of the end and will not prove false.*

*though it lingers, wait for it; it will certainly come and will not delay."*

It is so important that you record your dream. Not only will the written dream serve as a reminder to you of God's promise, it will also allow the right people to see your dream and assist you in fulfilling it. However, you must continually remember that the dream is for an appointed time, for God has to prepare you for your *Dream Fulfillment* by sending you on your *Journey.*

## *Reality*

The second area that has to be dealt with is reality. Let's examine the word reality. The root word of reality is real. The definition of *real* is "being an actual thing", having objective existence, or not imaginary. The suffix *ity* is used to form an abstract noun expressing a current state or condition. In examining the word real, I want to place emphasis on the phrase "objective existence." The word *objective* means dealing with what is external to the mind rather than with thoughts, feelings, or something existing independent of thought.

The problem that some people have with reality is that they allow their mind to form their reality based on their perception. Instead, they should be using their mind to navigate through the reality that naturally exists outside of their perception. Perception is based on your senses, experiences, and exposure to ideas. The inherent danger in always relying on perception is that when you have had limited exposure or no exposure to something, you may not be able to recognize it for what it truly is. Therefore, you should pray for godly discernment as you embark on your *Journey*. Godly discernment will never lead you wrong.

In the process of embarking on your *Journey*, you will have to face three reality checks: 1) selectively telling people about your dream, 2) standing strong when family and friends do not believe in your dream, and 3) staying away from those who conspire to kill your dream.

When you first receive your *Dream Presentation*, you are excited, and you feel like sharing it with the world or at a minimum your family and friends. However, you will quickly come to the realization that not everyone is going to receive your dream with the same excitement as you. Moreover, you will find that some of your family members and friends, whom you thought would rejoice with you, actually have disdain for your dream.

It is not that they do not love you or do not want you to succeed. They just do not want you to get ahead of their position in life or to outshine their endeavors. Look at the reaction that Joseph's brothers gave him. They thought Joseph was out of his mind when he told them about his dream. *"How dare he think that one day he would be in authority over us?"* Nevertheless, Joseph's dream came true, which means yours will too if you pursue it.

Before you tell anyone, pray about who needs to know about your dream. Not everyone who is close to you is ready to handle it. In doing so, you will eliminate a lot of unnecessary friction on your *Journey*.

If you have neglected to observe the first reality check, you will really have to adhere to the second one. Upon disclosing your *Dream Presentation* to a random group of family members and friends, you will quickly determine that you do not have everyone's support. After disclosing your dream, you may hear questions and statements that will be aimed at discouraging you from fulfilling your vision.

What makes you special enough to accomplish that dream? Where are you going to get the money to finance that endeavor? You do not have enough knowledge to produce that idea. No one in your family has ever accomplished that task. You will never be able to handle that career with the responsibility of raising your children. Can you develop that dream, and still handle your other responsibilities? What makes you think you can succeed in that industry?

In all of the questions and statements, notice how your dream was referred to as "that dream." This reference draws inference that the dream is not and cannot be yours. Those individuals making the statements are determined not to give you ownership of your dream. Hence, if you never own up to your dream, you will never claim and pursue your dream.

Therefore, you have to stand strong when your family and friends do not believe in your dream. Just as God told Joshua, *"Be strong and very courageous."* *(Joshua 1:7 –NKJV)* It is not easy facing the unknown especially if you have to do it by yourself, but if God has shown you what is to come, it is a done deal as long as you do not give up your pursuit.

Beyond the first two reality checks is the "granddaddy" of all the reality checks. Some people whom may encounter who will whole-heartedly seek to kill your dream. The person may be close to you or he or she may be someone who you never disclosed your heart's desire to. Somehow they heard about your endeavor while you were somewhere in the midst of your *Journey*. Nevertheless, a dream killer will do anything he or she deems necessary to stop you from fulfilling your dream.

Dream killers are usually individuals that are motivated by envy and fueled by selfishness. It is not that you have done anything to that person; rather it is the fact that you are seeking to accomplish something that they have not or cannot accomplish. I wish dream killers would realize that what has been ordained for you to accomplish has been assigned to you. I also pray that you realize that no one can stop you from fulfilling your dream except you.

Until a dream killer recognizes that what God has for you is indeed for you, it is in your best interest to avoid that person. Do not let your pride fool you into thinking that you have to stand and fight every adversary that crosses your path. Part of your *Journey* will be learning how to avoid the snares that seek to entrap you.

In 2 Chronicles 20:15, 17 (NIV), God told Jehoshaphat the following:

*"…Do not be afraid or discouraged because of this vast army.*

*For the battle is not yours, but God's.*

*You will not have to fight this battle. Take up your positions;*

*stand firm and see the deliverance the Lord will give you,*

*Judah and Jerusalem. Do not be afraid; do not be discouraged.*

*Go out to face them tomorrow, and the Lord will be with you."*

Even though your *Journey* is your process of maturing, God does not intend for you to die at the hand of a dream killer. Fight when God says fight, stand when God says stand, and walk away when God says leave something or someone alone.

# WE CAME TO CONQUER

I f your *Journey* has begun or if you are ready to begin it, your mind is probably all over the place with possibilities. However, in the back of your mind, you are probably thinking, *"Have I bitten off more than I can handle?" "Is my dream bigger than what I am capable of fulfilling?"* Stop! Cast those thoughts down! Focus! You are at one of the most pivotal points of your *Journey*.

I remember when I was the captain of my football team during my senior year in high school. My teammates and I had a dream to win the first championship in over twenty years for our high school. During that season, a few of my teammates and I had a saying that is applicable to this pivotal point of your *Journey*. When we faced a difficult situation on the field or in life, we would say, *"Will the fear override the hunger, or will the hunger override the fear?"* Translation: Are you going to let the fear of the unknown stop you from going after your dream? Whenever one of us asked that question, it was a trigger for the rest of us to "man-up" and focus on our dream. Needless to say, we won the championship that year. In all actuality, that accomplishment marks one of my first official *Journeys* in which I fulfilled a dream.

35

Much like my football championship trigger phrase, I found it useful to have a trigger phrase to help shake the fear out of my mind so I could continue moving towards my goal. Such a trigger is necessary because the *Journey* does gets difficult, especially once you enter into the *Wilderness March*. One of the greatest causes of a failed attempt at fulfilling a dream is having a mindset of fear. So just as a gun has a trigger that fires a bullet that kills, you need a trigger phrase or word that fires off a thought to kill the fear that builds up in your mind.

As a result, I created a trigger phrase that I use on all of my *Journeys*. My trigger phrase is *"We Came to Conquer"* which I also refer to as *"WCTC."* In the midst of a difficult *Journey*, this powerful phrase became a mantra that I lived by on a daily basis. It was so ingrained in my mind that it became a movement to propel me through the *Wilderness Marches* of my life. Hopefully, this movement will help propel you through your *Journey* as well.

The *"We Came to Conquer"* movement is a call to arms to fight against whatever is holding you back from reaching your full potential in every area of your life. In many cases, fear is the primary hindrance in our lives. However, our hindrances come in many forms. They can be a disability, family members, friends, finances, and (number one on the list) your mindset. However, you must stand up; take up the weapons needed for warfare, and fight against the obstacles that are keeping you from your dreams.

Notice I did not say, *"I Came to Conquer."* No one is able to complete his or her *Journey* alone. You will encounter individuals along your *Journey* who will help you in various ways. Just like a 16th Century King's army helping him conquer territory, these people will assist you on your *Journey* as you become a *Conqueror*.

In many instances, people tend to look at the word conquer in a military or a combative sense. However, a *Conqueror* is simply someone that overcomes obstacles. Again, on your *Journey* you will encounter many obstacles. In doing so, you will have to speak to the *Conqueror* inside of you, and tell him or her to fight. It is time to rule, subdue, and dominate your obstacles because the fulfillment of your dream hangs in the balance.

During the *Wilderness March*, when your *Journey* seems to be difficult, you will have to say to yourself, *Conquer!* When a clear vision of your dream seems to be disappearing, you will have to tell yourself, *Conquer!* When the resources needed to fulfill your dream seem to be drying up, you will have to remind yourself, *Conquer!* When everything else seems to be going awry, and your dream seems to be turning into a nightmare, do not give up. Stand up and yell, *Conquer! Conquer! Conquer! Conquer! Conquer!*

A *Conqueror's* mindset will prove to be invaluable as you enter the *Wilderness March* of your *Journey*. Without your Wilderness experience, your *Dream Fulfillment* will not manifest. It is your time of growth and maturation, so you can confidently and boldly walk in the fulfillment of your dream. It is time to become a *Successful Dreamer*. Just remember, *"We Came to Conquer."*

# STAGE II

# WILDERNESS MARCH

*Blind as I want to be, walking at Faith's pace,*

*My dream is laid out in front of me, completing my Journey will signal the end of my race.*

*There is a time and a season for everything under the sun,*

*I must constantly remind myself that my Journey has just begun.*

*Fear will come knocking and challenges will stop by,*

*I will just stand tall yelling out my Conqueror's War Cry.*

*My battle wounds may run deep, and scars may be long,*

*Yet I will walk into my Dream Fulfillment matured and standing strong.*

*The Wilderness March of my Journey is necessary to go through,*

*In the end, I will say, "God, well worth it! Thank you!"*

Your "jungle swagger" has been activated; your mind is engaged and focused on your *Journey* ahead. Now it is time to enter your *Wilderness March*.

Before we go any further, let's look at the word wilderness. It means an unsettled, uncultivated region left in its natural condition. An example is a large wild tract of land covered with forest. Another example is an extensive area such as a desert or ocean that is barren or empty. Even though these geographical areas are common around the world, not many people venture into them. Most people just ride by them, fly over them, or sail across them. For the most part, the common person does not want to enter into the wilderness. However, to be a *Successful Dreamer*, you will have to go through the *Wilderness*.

Just as some negative actions and reactions that are perceived to be negative are necessary, the *Wilderness March* of your *Journey* is necessary. It prepares you to fulfill your dreams. Within your dream, you will need certain skills and abilities, but you may not currently possess them. However, your *Wilderness March* is designed to afford you the opportunity to acquire what you need. Do you lack patience? If so, you may experience trials and tribulations that will develop your patience. Perhaps your dream will require you to be a strong administrator. Therefore, you may have to take a path that requires you to work in various administrative positions. Whatever you need will be developed during your *Wilderness March*.

## INTERCONNECTIVITY OF YOUR JOURNEYS

One thing you need to know about the *Journey of a Successful Dreamer* is that you will go through many *Journeys* in your life. Some of them will be small while others will be large. At the completion of each one, you will reach a *Dream Fulfillment*. These prerequisite *Journeys* you go through are in direct correlation with the acronym *C.H.A.N.G.E.* (Complete Happiness After Never Giving-up Expectations) that I used earlier. The key to changing is never giving up on what you expect to obtain. However, your expectations have to be accomplished through calculated and obtainable steps.

39

Much in the same way is the *Journey of a Successful Dreamer*. The sum of all the skills and abilities learned after completing each *Journey* equals the total preparation you will need to fulfill your destiny in life. Your destiny is your purpose in life which God placed in you at birth to accomplish while you are here on earth. However, your skills and talents have to be developed over a period of time. It is next to impossible to develop into the person your destiny is calling you to be using a "microwave approach." Ecclesiastes 3:1 *(NKJV)* states:

*"To everything there is a season,*

*a time for every purpose under heaven:"*

Therefore, there is a time and season for you to acquire certain skills and talents. God's appointed time to release you into your purpose will determine the time and season of your maturation. When it is all said and done, you will be able to reflect over your life and see how each *Journey* is connected, like the gears of a clock or the pieces of a puzzle.

## THE GEARS OF LIFE

Have you ever looked inside a grandfather clock? It is full of interlinked gears that are interdependent in an effort to keep the clock displaying accurate time. That is the ultimate purpose of the clock. Some of the gears are small and some are large. However, in the grand scheme or purpose of the clock, the size of the gears does not matter. Each gear has its individual purpose, so to fulfill the purpose of the clock, each one has to do what it was created to do. If each gear does not fulfill its function, the purpose of the clock will be hindered or stopped.

In the same sense, your various *Journeys* are like the gears of your life. The timetable that is being kept was set forth by God before He spoke the words *"Let there be light"* in Genesis. Your *Journeys* are the interlinked and interdependent gears of your purpose. God actually created each one of us with a destiny that is interconnected with the completion of each *Journey*.

Some of them are large and some are small. Nevertheless it takes the skills and talents acquired from each of them to fulfill our purpose in life.

At the appointed time, each gear turns to fulfill its purpose. As a result of their interconnectivity, the adjacent gear's purpose starts as soon as the first one's movement pushes it into action. If the first one does not turn, then the next movement will not begin. If the second gear, somehow, begins to turn before the first one, then it can cause damage to the clock. Therefore, each gear has to wait for its appointed time to move.

In much the same way, your *Journeys* are for an appointed time, so you can fulfill our purpose. During one season of your life, your *Journey* may be established for you to acquire patience. As such, you may be placed in a stressful and demanding administrative job. If you do not gain the ability to be patient before you enter the administrative job, your success in that job will be hindered, delayed, or destroyed. Therefore, the success of future *Journeys* depends on the success of the current *Journey*.

## MY PERSONAL EXPERIENCE

I can clearly remember one of the most important *Journeys* in my life thus far. My experience during the *Wilderness March* of this *Journey* definitely led me down the *Forest Path* and the *Desert Path*. I will talk more about both of these paths later.

Just as most people would be, I was excited when I received my *Dream Presentation*. It revealed to me that I would be teaching and empowering people to succeed, which I thought was great. I looked at this revelation as a natural progression of whom God had made me. However, I had no idea of what was required for me to reach my *Dream Fulfillment*.

In the midst of my *Wilderness March*, it seemed to me that I had hit a wall. I had clearly gone down the *Forest Path*, but now I was experiencing a dry season on the *Desert Path*. My wife and I had lost most of our real estate assets, and our finances were in dire straits. Someone looking at us from the outside would have never known the type of season we were going through.

We were in the midst of a financial upheaval. God had orchestrated a series of financial events that were necessary for us to endure to acquire what was needed to walk into the fulfillment of the dream. I remember riding home one afternoon during that season of my life, having a conversation with God. *When will this season end? Am I doing something wrong? Is there something I need to do differently? Lord, please forgive me for anything I have done, or I am still doing wrong."* Shortly after I finished my ranting, God gave me the following vision:

*I was in the middle of the ocean, totally surrounded by water. I do not know how long I had been swimming out to sea, but I could not see land anywhere. However, I seemed to be standing on a sandbar that was high enough to keep my nose just above the water. I was obviously tired, and I was thinking that I should turn around and go back in the direction that I started.*

*Suddenly, God spoke to me and said, "You do not have enough energy to go back to where you started. You only have enough energy to get to where I am sending you."* As I listened, the vision continued. God said, *"If you take a step away from where I have placed you, you could fall into a sinkhole and perish. If you perish, you will never partake of all the things I have prepared for you at the end of your Journey."* As I came back to reality and continued my drive home, I felt so encouraged and ready to continue.

As powerful as this vision was to me, it was not complete. Several months later, God showed me more. The rest of the vision came to me about thirty minutes before I was scheduled to give a keynote address at an event. In all actuality, the keynote address was on the *Journey of a Successful Dreamer*. At the pre-mixer of the event, I was talking to a young man whom I had not seen in several months. I was telling him about my "middle of the ocean" vision. Suddenly, during our conversation, God revealed the rest of the vision to me. It was a follows:

*God showed me that while I was thinking that I was just stuck on a sandbar in the middle of the ocean, He was preparing a wave that would take me to my destination. This wave was going to wash me on to the shores of the people who need my skills and services.*

42

At first, I did not understand what God was showing me, but He soon gave me clarity.

Think about it. An ocean brings nutrients to people on the coast, i.e. food and water. However, a process of cleaning and preparation must be completed before any nutrients from the ocean can be served to people. A fish out of water has to be scaled, cleaned, and cooked before it can be given to people to eat. In much the same way, you will have to be cleaned up after your *Wilderness March*. As you land on the shore of your destiny, you will be slightly disoriented and covered with the dirt of your *Journey*. You will have to take a moment and acclimate yourself to your new environment. Once you have gotten your bearings, you will notice that the people in need of what you have to offer will be ready for you to walk in your purpose.

That revelation spoke volumes to me, so I shared it with the young man at the event. As I was doing so, I recalled that this is essentially what happened to Joseph. Before Joseph dwelled in the Palace, God allowed him to be placed in a prison for several years. Meanwhile, He orchestrated a wave of events that landed Joseph in the Palace where he was needed.

While Joseph was in the prison, he met Pharaoh's butler. Eventually, his relationship with the butler afforded him the opportunity to go before the king of Egypt, who needed his skills. However, Joseph had to be cleaned up before he entered his presence. He had to get the dirt and the stench of the prison off of himself. Once he went before Pharaoh to exercise his gift, he walked into his destiny and started fulfilling his purpose. Henceforth, Joseph had reached his *Dream Fulfillment*.

As a result of this revelation, I realized even more that the things my wife and had gone through were necessary. How could I effectively motivate, educate, and empower someone to fulfill their destiny if I had never experienced life-altering challenges before reaching my own destiny? It would be like someone who has never earned a million dollars teaching you a sure-fire method to earning a million dollars. Because I have navigated and completed the *Journey of a Successful Dreamer*, I can now teach you how to navigate the *Journey*.

# THE FOREST PATH

We have all heard of the saying "the lesser of two evils" which is how some people may describe the *Forest Path* of the *Journey of a Successful Dreamer*. However, the *Forest Path* is not evil. It may not be a situation you want to go through, but it may be necessary. When you enter the *Wilderness March*, your destination will prescribe one of two paths. You will walk down the *Forest Path* or the *Desert Path*, sometimes both. Your path selection is made based on the knowledge and level of maturity needed to reach your *Dream Fulfillment*.

As discussed earlier in the radio station analogy, sometimes you venture into the opposite direction of your dream. As a result, you have to be redirected back into the right position. Sometimes you have to endure some drastic changes to get back on track with God's plan and timetable for your purpose. The depth in which you stray off course will also have a bearing on the experiences you will encounter on either path.

Just as the title suggests, the *Forest Path* emulates the conditions found in a natural forest which contains many signs of life. A forest has streams and rivers of water, plants and vegetation, and a multitude of animals and insects. In comparison, many signs of your dream becoming a reality begin to appear when you are on the *Forest Path*. God will provide many opportunities or avenues for you to fulfill your dream. You will see potential streams of income, funding sources, human resources, and other resources needed for your dream to survive. However, all of this comes with a cost. Remember, it is survival of the fittest. You will have to fight and endure challenges to get what you need to become a *Successful Dreamer*.

Your fight to become a *Successful Dreamer* will not always be to the death, metaphorically speaking. Remember, your *Wilderness March* will present opportunities and avenues for you to acquire needed skills and/or a certain level of maturity. If you think about the forest, notice that it presents various levels of challenges. Sometimes the only obstacle that stands between you and what you need is a spider on its web. On the other hand, you may have to face off with a grizzly bear to reach your goal. In regard to the *Forest Path*, you may have to face an obstacle as simple as passing a certification test or something as arduous as raising the capital needed to launch a business. However, what you need is obtainable; you can actually see it. Nevertheless, you will have to conquer some type of impediment to acquire what you need.

As you walk the *Forest Path*, it is important to remember that it is not just about conquering the obstacle to reach your goal. An important aspect of the *Forest Path* is learning the proper manner to overcome your obstacle. Think of it this way. In a natural forest, all living organisms grow or mature according to how they respond to their surroundings. For example, let us examine forest plants. If several types of plants are in the same patch of ground, one of three things will probably happen. Some of the plants will be smothered and die, some plants will grow but be dominated by stronger plants, or some plants will grow harmoniously together. In order to become a *Successful Dreamer*, you have to strive to respond in the best manner to your surroundings and overcome challenges as they emerge. Your response will determine how long you stay on the *Path*.

Another aspect of the forest that needs to be discussed is the danger that exists. Within a forest, many dangers such as snake pits and poisonous vegetation abound. Each one of these dangers is lethal in its own right and needs to be avoided. On the *Forest Path*, you will find similar dangers. Instead of a snake pit, you may allow your dreams to fall into a den of thieves who will rob you of any hope of reaching your *Dream Fulfillment*. Instead of poisonous vegetation, you will run into individuals who want to poison your mind to corrupt your dream.

When I think about the *Forest Path*, the words of the song "The Message," written by Grandmaster Flash, comes to mind:

*"Don't push me 'cuz I'm close to the edge*

*I'm trying not to lose my head*

*Uh huh ha ha ha*

*It's like a jungle sometimes*

*It makes me wonder how I keep from goin under."*

As you go down the *Forest Path*, you will encounter many situations that will make you feel like giving up because you are tired of fighting. However, you have to keep telling yourself, "I must stay strong in the pursuit of my dream and endure to the end."

# THE DESERT PATH

The *Forest Path* can be a difficult way to travel, but the *Desert Path* will take your *Wilderness March* to another level of intensity. The *Forest Path* is full of challenges that can place you in close proximity to the resources you need. However, the *Desert Path* can isolate you from those same resources.

Think about the elements of a natural desert. It is essentially the opposite of a forest in many negative ways. In a desert, there are not many signs of life, whereas a forest has many signs of life. The desert, by definition is a dry place, whereas a forest has streams, rivers, and other sources of moisture. Another major difference between a desert and a forest is the lack of options or opportunities in a desert to obtain nourishment for your body.

When your *Wilderness March* takes you down the *Desert Path*, you will find that this path emulates the natural desert. It will appear to you that the possibility of your dream becoming a reality is fading away. The options and avenues that you once saw will start disappearing. When you walk through the natural desert, all you will see is sand. You will not identify many signs of life. You may encounter skeletal remains of various animals signifying that they also journeyed this way but did not survive. It is much the same on the *Desert Path*. You may run into the skeletal remains of other people's dreams that died in the *Wilderness*.

In the desert, the vastness of the dry sand represents the dryness that you start experiencing in regard to your skills and resources. It may appear that you are having challenges with the skills that once flourished for you. It also appears that your resources are drying up; the money that you once had access to is gone. The people that were once committed to your dream may begin to leave you stranded. Your dream may appear to be withering away in front of your eyes without having any ability to stop it.

As you continue your walk down the *Desert Path*, you may grow weary. Consequently, you may start to give up hope which is a dangerous place to be. Resultantly, your vision starts to become cloudy and your judgment starts to falter, causing you to see mirages. You may think you are seeing a body of water or people coming to help you. In all actuality, the body of water may be the edge of a cliff, and the rescuers may be a pit of snakes.

Mirages are seen on the *Desert Path* when you place your hope in people and situations that appear to be real but are not. These people or situations beguile you into trusting them because you think you have no other hope. As a result, your dream receives fatal blows and dies in the *Wilderness*.

Remember, the *Desert Path* exists to build your faith in your dream, mature you, and build your skills and abilities even more than the *Forest Path*. The depth of your *Wilderness* experience is a good indicator of the depth of your dream and purpose. In the *Wilderness*, your survival will leave you well prepared to walk into your *Dream Fulfillment*. Even though everything around you is indicating that your dream is dying, causing all hope to be lost, you have to rely on your inner most faith and believe that if God said it, that settles it. Go through your *Wilderness March*; your success is just ahead of you!

## YOUR WILDERNESS DECREE

Yes, the *Wilderness March* can be a beast. When you are in the middle of it, sometimes no amount of words of encouragement seem to be enough. In the back of your mind, you will think that no one understands what you are going through. Truth be told, no one will understand your complete *Journey*. It was created especially for you to gain maturity, knowledge, or needed skills to fulfill your dream. Sometimes, therefore, you will have to encourage yourself as you continue your *Journey*.

One great source of encouragement on my *Wilderness Marches* has been a decree that summarizes the *Journey of a Successful Dreamer*. The decree simply states:

"**FAITH** in my dream along with the proper **ATTITUDE**

builds the **CHARACTER** needed to resist **SEDUCTION**

and survive **PERIODS OF LACK** as my **PREPARATION**

meets the **FAVOR** and **OPPORTUNITY** needed to

preempt the **DEATH** of my dream."

Each of the words in bold contains a key ingredient to the success of your dream. Let us examine each one.

## *Faith*

While you are on your *Wilderness March*, you will need two categories of faith. First, you must have faith in your dream. You have to believe that in spite of what situation crosses your path, your dream is going to come to fruition. Next, you have to be faithful over your current assignment. Even if your current assignment seems to be the farthest thing away from fulfilling your dream, do it to the best of your ability. Treat it as if you were operating in the culmination of your dream. You never know when you will enter the presence of the person or people who will help you achieve your dream.

## *Attitude*

When you are in the *Wilderness March*, you will mature based on how you respond to situations you encounter. Therefore, your attitude is an integral part of your success. When life is not going the way you prefer, will you exhibit a good attitude or a bad attitude? Even though you may be struggling through your situation, will you still take time to help someone else who is in need? When your world has turned upside down, will you still smile and give God the glory, or will you frown and say, "Woe is me?" When your attitude is good, then you will mature and learn necessary lessons as you go through your situations. If your attitude is bad, you may have to repeat the same situation until you go through it with the proper attitude. Good attitude – blessings abound. Bad attitude – blessings deferred. Which do you prefer?

## Character

Character is something that is built over time because it has to be developed. It is what defines you; it is not what you do, such as a vocation or role. It is the internal house that defines your integrity. I describe integrity as a house because of their similarities. A house can be beautiful on the outside, but its structural integrity may be in a state of decay. In much the same way, you may be beautiful on the outside, but your soul may be rotting. During the *Wilderness March,* your integrity will be tested. The results of your test will determine how much character building you will need to strengthen your integrity.

Sometimes, character needs minor repairs. Sometimes, it needs a face-lift. Sometimes, it needs to be gutted to the framework and rebuilt. Other times, it needs to be demolished and a different character needs to be built in its place. As you go through the *Wilderness March,* your character will be developed and refined to become what it needs to be to walk into your *Dream Fulfillment.*

## Seduction

Seduction is not always about the lust of the flesh and your sexual gratification. It is simply the act of luring or persuading you to do acts you would not normally do or did not plan to do. Usually, it is a lure to do acts that benefits someone other than you. In the *Wilderness March,* you will encounter people or situations that are enticing, but your interaction with these people or situations will not be beneficial to the fulfillment of your dream.

Even though Joseph's seduction was in a sexual nature, it was a metaphor for the types of seduction that you can encounter. If Joseph would have relaxed his morals by giving into the seduction from Potiphar's wife, he would have never been placed in position to ascend to the palace. Do not fall prey to the superficial gratification that seduction will supply. A temporary moment of pleasure, be it of the flesh, monetary, or otherwise, is not worth being thrown off your path to your destiny. Every nut is not worth the squirrel's chase. Stay your course and experience true gratification, your *Dream Fulfillment.*

## Periods of Lack

Matthew 16:26 (NKJV) states:

*"For what profit is it to a man if he gains the whole world, and loses his own soul?*

*Or what will a man give in exchange for his soul?"*

The soul is one of the innermost parts of a person containing the thoughts and desires that are connected to your dream. The above scripture is applicable to the experience on the *Wilderness March.*

As you go through life, you will acquire many belongings. You may hold some of these items near and dear to your heart, and never foresee any event that might separate you from them. However, your *Wilderness March* will produce events that may lead to the loss of some or all of those possessions. This is not a good feeling. I have actually been in a *Wilderness March* where my wife and I lost a great deal of our possessions.

When you are in the midst of your *Wilderness March,* you may not see the big picture of your *Journey.* Please understand that God is working every situation out for your good. Such trials and tribulations occur to build your faith and make you mentally stronger. In addition, they eliminate unnecessary distractions so you can focus on your dream. You may lose money, property, and friends, but do not lose focus of your dream. The fulfillment of your dream can afford you exceedingly and abundantly more than what you lose during your *Wilderness March*.

## Preparation

If I could summarize the *Wilderness March* in one word, I would say it is preparation. The entire focus of this part of your *Journey* is to prepare you for your *Dream Fulfillment*. As you go through this period of preparation, you will discover certain gifts you have. Also during this period, certain talents will be developed. Your level of preparation during the *Wilderness March* will depend on the level of transition needed to move you from who you are at *Dream Presentation* to who you will have become at *Dream Fulfillment*.

Remember, you will go through many *Journeys* in your lifetime. Some of them will be long; some of them will be short. Some of them will be painful; some of them will be painless. Some of them will be life changing; some of them will be at most educational. Nevertheless, your sum total of experiences on all of your *Journeys* will equal what you need to fulfill your purpose in life. Although it may take a lifetime to prepare, it only takes a moment to execute.

## Favor

A common phrase that some people use is "favor isn't fair." However, I beg to differ. Favor is fair. The amount of favor a person receives can be gauged by how closely they follow their assigned path in life. It is not necessarily how well they do on their path. Within that gauge is a calibration tool, which is your heart. Not your physical heart, but your emotional and mental one. In spite of how well you navigate your *Wilderness March*, what is the intent of your heart? Are your strides based on self-gain, or do you seek to help others as you walk your path? Fortunately for you, only God can truly judge your intent.

Nevertheless, God will show you grace as you travel toward your dream. Grace is God's unmerited favor. Even though you may make mistakes that disqualify you from your dream, God allows you a chance to restart and finish it. That is partially why the *Wilderness March* exists. In your immaturity, you may have strayed away from your *Dream Fulfillment*. However, the preparation you go through matures you, so you can fulfill your dream. It is your chance to walk in what God promised you before you were formed in your mother's womb.

Not only does God give you grace, He also places people in your life to show you kindness as well. In situations when you least expect, God will assign someone to extend you favor in an area of need. It could come in the area of finances, education, employment, etc. God will use someone to provide a need or even a desire when you least expect that need or desire to be fulfilled. Your faithfulness in completing your assigned path will gain you more favor than you could ever imagine.

## *Opportunity*

A wise person once said, "Success comes when preparation meets opportunity." I also like a few quotes from Confucius, the Chinese philosopher. Confucius stated, "Success depends upon previous preparation, and without such preparation there is sure to be failure." He also stated, "The superior man makes the difficulty to be overcome his first interest; success only comes later." These quotes have so much depth, and are applicable to the Wilderness March.

Even though you may receive the vision of your dream all in one night, becoming a Successful Dreamer does not happen overnight. It is a process of preparing and maturing. As you go through your Wilderness March, your experiences enable you to realize your gifts and talents. Your Wilderness March also matures you, so that you are able to properly handle and/or utilize those attributes. Once this occurs, you will be ready for the opportunities that will present themselves to you. If you do not go through your Wilderness March, you will not be prepared for opportunity's knock on your door.

Proverbs 18:16 (NKJV) states the following:

*"A man's gift makes room for him,*

*and brings him before great men."*

This scripture is on point. Look at the life of Joseph in addition to the many dreamers that come after him. Even though he was in prison, his gift, which was developed in the *Wilderness*, brought him before a great man, Pharaoh. Ultimately, his gift made room for him to become second in charge in Egypt.

Another important note should be taken from Joseph's appointment with opportunity. Because He had been in prison for so long, he cleaned up himself prior to going before Pharaoh. When you are in your *Wilderness March*, you can become rough in your appearance. You have to make it a point to become presentable once again. Do not let a rough exterior prevent people from seeing and being blessed by what you have to offer. A first impression can be the lasting impression.

The *Wilderness March* is a trial that you have to pass. After the trial, opportunity comes knocking because you have proven that you are ready. When it comes, promotion will follow. All it takes is one open door to allow you to realize your destiny. Do not miss this chance because you are not prepared.

## *Death*

Lastly, you must remember that you cannot allow other people's death wish for your dream deter you from completing your *Journey*. People will plot against you attempting to set you up for failure. You must know that no man can snatch you out of the hand of God. Even though the *Wilderness March* can be rough, you are still under God's protection. He is orchestrating your life to bring you to a point of maturity. What the devil thinks he is using to destroy you will be used by God to bless you if you maintain your faith by staying on your path.

When you walk through the *Wilderness*, you will encounter mirage moments. Do not let those perceived, albeit false moments of breakthrough become a breakdown. Use them to catapult toward your *Journey's* end. The power of life and death are in your tongue. Speak death to your obstacles and life to your dreams.

## WILDERNESS MARCH CONCLUSION

The *Wilderness March* is a period of preparation leading to your maturity. Unfortunately, this period sometimes gives the perception that your dream is being denied. Nevertheless, it is the most important part of your *Journey*. During the *Wilderness March*, you will either blossom and mature into your dream, or you will wither up and kill your dream. The choice is all yours!

# STAGE III

# DREAM FULFILLMENT

The resounding question in your mind is probably, "How do I know when I am out of the Wilderness?" When God revealed the process of the *Journey of a Successful Dreamer* to me, God had to tell me when I had exited the *Wilderness March*. It was not because the situations in my life still had a *Wilderness* feel; it was because my understanding of walking in my *Dream Fulfillment* did not fit God's definition. I was metaphorically expecting to be running with my vision and not crawling with my vision.

## WALKING IN YOUR DREAM FULFILLMENT

One day I was driving around running errands. At the same time, I was talking to God saying, *"I will really be glad when my Dream Fulfillment comes."* This conversation actually occurred during the life-changing *Journey* I previously talked about. Immediately, God spoke to my spirit and said, *"You are already in the Dream Fulfillment phase of your Journey."*

I started thinking, *"How is that so? I am still working a 9 to 5 job that I am ready to leave. My financial situation still has not recovered. Things are not going how I envisioned them to be in Dream Fulfillment."* Of course, the problem was that I did not see my life the way God saw it. After that light bulb flashed on, God showed me the revelation of walking in *Dream Fulfillment*.

During this *Journey*, my *Dream Presentation* was my work career changing from nine to five employment to becoming the entrepreneur that God had placed in my spirit before I reached the age of ten. I came to the realization that I had been on this *Journey* since I first received the dream. God had me on a series of smaller *Journeys* to get me to a place where I was able to operate as an entrepreneur. The problem was that my concept of a businessman was one who was working full-time in his own business.

God told me that I was walking in my dream already because I owned and operated a part-time business. As a matter of fact, most of the people in the community who knew of me already thought I was a full-time entrepreneur. God continued by telling me that I was already offering some of the services that I had envisioned. However, my short sightedness expected *Dream Fulfillment* to automatically come with the full-time business and the income to match. Boy, was I wrong.

## WALKING BEFORE YOU RUN

What I now realize is that *Dream Fulfillment* is a buildup process. It is literally walking before you run, emulating the stages of a baby learning to walk. Before a baby can walk, it has to learn how to stand on its own. Once he or she learns how to stand, then the process of learning how to walk can begin. If you can envision this example, you will recall the tiny baby steps. These steps are what you experience when you first start walking in your dream. As a baby gets used to walking, he or she will start walking a little faster, eventually reaching a normal walking pace. Once you get used to operating in your dream, you will start operating as if it was always a part of your life. The last stage with a baby is when he or she gets comfortable walking and becomes able to lift its knees higher and run. Once your dream becomes second nature to you, you will be able to run with your dream and experience all that God has in store for you.

Even though your dream may start at a slow pace, it can accelerate from zero to sixty like a car. However, God determines your point and rate of acceleration. A Ford Mustang GT will go from zero to sixty miles per hour (mph) in about 4.5 seconds. A Honda Accord will go from zero to sixty mph in about 7.3 seconds. Once the Accord gets to sixty mph, the rate of both cars is exactly the same. In other words, although it might take you a little longer to achieve the same level of operation within your dream as someone else, the level of operation is the same in the end.

Do not mistake what I am saying as a competition. It is all about maximizing what God has called you to do. The point is not to become dismayed because the fulfillment of your dream takes longer to manifest than someone else's dream. Just sit back, fasten your seatbelt, and enjoy the ride. God has a lot in store for you; plus, the scenery is wonderful.

## PIECING THE PUZZLE TOGETHER

As you walk in your dream, you will start recognizing why you encountered certain experiences on your *Wilderness March*. Situations may have occurred during your *Wilderness March* that will make you cry out, *"Why me? What does this have to do with my dream?"* In the words of the old gospel songwriter, Charles A. Tindley:

*"By and by Lord, when the morning comes,*

*When the saints of God are gathered home together as one,*

*We'll tell the story how we've overcome,*

*For we'll understand it better by and by."*

That is right! You will understand it better as you fulfill your *Journey*. Keep in mind that all of the situations you will encounter will not be bad. They may just leave a question in your mind. *"How does this fit into my purpose?"*

In 1996, I was a member of a church where I was heavily involved in ministry work. My Pastor, Dr. Norris D. Darden, Jr., would ask me to lead various ministries because of my gift of administration and leadership. One of the ministries that I led was the Media Ministry, which included all audio and visual elements of the church. One of the biggest parts of that ministry was the television broadcast that we produced. The interesting part about this assignment was that I had no audio or video experience. However, I followed one of the first rules of the *Journey of a Successful Dreamer*. I embraced my current assignment and fulfilled it to the best of my ability.

Of course, my ability at that time was not much since I had no prior experience. Nevertheless, I became a student and a leader. I have a philosophy that in order to effectively lead, one must first learn about what he is leading. In addition, when God places you on an assignment, He will make provisions for you to fulfill it. Remember, your current assignment is all about learning skills and gaining experience to fulfill your dream.

When I took over the Media Ministry, God had already placed someone there who could teach me what I needed to know. That person was Arcelious Daniels, a great teacher. At that time, he was completing his Master's Degree in Film and Television from the Savannah College of Art and Design. He taught me the basics of sound and video. Soon I became so adept at learning that he kept teaching me more and more of his knowledge. To make a long story short, Arcelious and I became like brothers. We even started a video and film production company together with our wives. Through that company, I became a filmmaker by directing and producing my first independent documentary film called *Stubborn as A Mule*.

The production of *Stubborn as A Mule* was a journey in itself. I will have to tell you about that in a book of its own because it took nine years to complete. Nevertheless, during the writing of this book, the documentary was garnering great reviews by such intellectual luminaries as Dr. Cornel West. If I had never embraced my assignment as Director of the Media Ministry, I would probably not be a filmmaker today. Filmmaking was not something I envisioned until my gift was activated. In the words of Dr. West after he saw the documentary, *"Wow! What a God we serve!"* That piece of the puzzle to my purpose may not have fallen in place if I did not accepted my Media Ministry assignment. In hindsight, I can see that now.

From the *Dream Presentation* of *Stubborn as a Mule* through the *Wilderness March* of its production, my skills as a director and producer matured as I became a filmmaker in my *Dream Fulfillment*. The documentary has become an internationally award-winning film receiving awards in Africa, the United Kingdom, Germany, and the United States.

## DREAM RESPONSIBILITY

As you operate in your dream, you will have many responsibilities. However, two indirect responsibilities are needed to maintain your dream. The normal responsibilities would be tasks like properly operating your business, continually sharpening your skill set, continual education, financial stewardship, and prayer to name a few. The two additional responsibilities are being a blessing to others and forgiving those who treated you unfairly on your *Journey*.

In a society such as ours, you will find that some people are less likely to help others once they fulfill their dream. Such people adopt the "I got mine, you get yours" attitude. However, a true *Successful Dreamer* should never have that attitude. A *Successful Dreamer* should always be willing and have a desire to help others, not just in life issues, but also in the pursuit of their dream. Just as God placed people in your life to assist you on your *Journey*, God will place you in someone's path to help them. You will find that the more you help others, the more others will help you even after you have fulfilled your dream.

The other responsibility is to forgive those who placed obstacles in your path. Even though Joseph would have probably been justified in unfairly treating his brothers during the great famine, he chose to bless them instead. As he forgave his brothers, God restored his relationship with his family after many years of disconnection. Through Joseph's forgiveness, his *Dream Fulfillment* was able to go to another level. He fulfilled his major purpose in life. Through all his many *Journeys* from the pit to the palace, Joseph matured and acquired everything he needed to save the lives of his people, the Israelites. If he had never gone through his *Journey* to become second in command in Egypt, the Israelites may have starved to death.

What is on the other side of your *Dream Fulfillment*? What part of your purpose's puzzle is hanging in the balance waiting on the completion of your current *Journey*? Maintaining an unforgiving heart can prevent you from maximizing the results of your *Journey*, severely hindering your ultimate purpose. As hard as it may be, the responsibility of forgiveness is yours.

## I AM A SUCCESSFUL DREAMER

Although the *Journey of a Successful Dreamer* is not easy, it is worth it. As I look back over my life, I see the many small, medium, and large *Journeys* that have made me who I am. I see the times when my quests were hard; I see the times when they were good. I think about all the skills I have acquired, the lessons I have learned, and the maturity I have gained.

I can truly say that because I have embraced all of my assignments and completed them to the best of my ability, many doors of favor have opened for me. At the end of the day I can truly say God has kept me from many toils and snares. Even though I have seen the valley, God allowed me to walk though it and not stay. The *Wilderness Marches* of my life have made me strong, so now I am fit to carry out the destiny that is in front of me.

In hindsight of all my *Journeys* thus far, I can still say I would rather experience trials and tribulations in the pursuit of my dream than to live the nightmare of a dream not pursued. A dream deferred is a future nightmare.

Become a *Successful Dreamer* by starting your *Journey* today. Look into your mirror and speak life into your dream. Take a deep breath – exhale – and speak the following words:

# I AM A SUCCESSFUL DREAMER

CPSIA information can be obtained
at www.ICGtesting.com
Printed in the USA
JSHW050720151220
10147JS00007B/19